X-Treme Sports

Skateboarding

K.E. Vieregger

ABDO Publishing Company

visit us at
www.abdopub.com

Published by ABDO Publishing Company, 4940 Viking Drive, Edina, Minnesota 55435.
Copyright © 2003 by Abdo Consulting Group, Inc. International copyrights reserved in all
countries. No part of this book may be reproduced in any form without written permission from
the publisher.

Printed in the United States.

Cover Photo: Corbis
Interior Photos: Corbis pp. 5, 6, 7, 9, 10, 11, 13, 14, 15, 16, 17, 19, 22-23, 24, 25, 26, 27, 28, 29, 31

Editors: Kate A. Conley, Stephanie Hedlund, Jennifer R. Krueger
Art Direction: Neil Klinepier

Library of Congress Cataloging-in-Publication Data

Vieregger, K. E., 1978-
  Skateboarding / K. E. Vieregger.
     p. cm. -- (X-treme sports)
  Includes index.
  Summary: Examines the history, equipment, techniques and games, and more of skateboarding.
  ISBN 1-57765-928-7
  1. Skateboarding--Juvenile literature. [1. Skateboarding.] I. Title. II. Title: Skate boarding. III.
  Series.

GV859.8 .V83 2003
796.22--dc21
                                                                        2002026094

Contents

Skateboarding

Skateboarding first became popular about 40 years ago. The sport has changed a lot since then. But it still remains a great way to exercise and have fun.

Anyone can learn to skateboard. Protective gear and a skateboard are the only pieces of equipment you need. Once you get started, it can be fun to practice and perform tricks with friends, family, or even by yourself.

Talented skateboarders learn tricks that can be dangerous. However, skateboarding is one of the safest sports to learn. With proper training, you can learn skateboarding skills that you can enjoy for years.

Television, magazines, and books have increased skateboarding's popularity. Today, skateboarding is an exciting sport with local and international competitions. In 2002, more than 20 million people worldwide enjoyed this sport.

Sidewalk Surfing

Skateboarding first became popular in the early 1960s. Surfers in southern California were the first to use skateboards. They wanted something to do when the ocean was too calm to surf. The first skateboards looked like little surfboards. So skateboarding was called sidewalk surfing.

At first, some people made their own skateboards. They took the wheels off roller skates and attached them to pieces of wood. Skateboards were also sold in stores. But they were expensive and could be dangerous.

By 1965, about 50 million skateboards had been sold in the United States. These early skateboards looked different from today's boards. They had clay or steel wheels. These wheels did not turn easily or offer support on bumpy surfaces. The boards were small, flat, and unstable. This made performing **stunts** difficult. Even worse, the boards often broke after landing minor jumps. For these and other reasons, skateboarding's popularity lessened in the late 1960s.

In 1970, a California surfer named Frank Nasworthy visited a plastics factory. The factory made **urethane** wheels for roller skates. Nasworthy thought these wheels would work better on a skateboard than the clay or steel wheels. The new wheels absorbed the **shock** of riding much better.

Nasworthy began promoting the new wheels in California. Then in 1973, a new skateboard was introduced. It had urethane wheels and a more advanced board design. Now skateboarding was easier and more fun. Skateboarding once again became popular.

During the 1970s, skateparks were everywhere. But by the 1980s, many had closed. Those that remained open were poorly maintained. So skaters decided to skate in the streets and in abandoned swimming pools instead.

Then in 1995, skateboarding received lots of attention. That's because it was part of ESPN's first-ever Extreme Games, which are now called the X Games. Soon, a new generation of skateboarding began. People from all over the world were hopping on boards and learning to skate!

Opposite page: Many new skateparks have been developed since the ESPN Extreme Games in 1995. Many have ramps similar to this one.

Gear

Skateboarders need only two things to get rolling. They need protective gear and a skateboard. It is a good idea to purchase these items at the same time and keep them together. This makes it easy to remember to wear the protective gear.

Skateboarders should wear long-sleeved shirts and long pants. This clothing will protect a skateboarder's skin from scrapes. Skateboarders should also wear rubber-soled shoes. These shoes have a good grip, which keeps the skater from slipping off the board. In addition, skateboarders should always wear gloves, knee pads, elbow pads, and a helmet. This gear protects skateboarders from injuries. For this reason, it should be worn at all times.

The only other gear needed is a skateboard. It is often best for a beginner to purchase an inexpensive board. However, a skater should not buy the cheapest board available. That is because a skateboard made of poor-quality materials can be dangerous.

The Setup

Skateboard designs vary with the style of skating. But all skateboards have four parts. These parts are the deck, trucks, wheels, and **bearings**. Together, these parts are called the setup.

The main part of the setup is the deck. This is where skaters put their feet. The front of the deck is the nose, and the back of the deck is the tail. Often, skateboard manufacturers print colorful designs on the bottoms of the decks. Skaters also put stickers on their decks to make them **unique**.

On the bottom of the deck are the trucks. Trucks fasten the wheels to the skateboard. They also allow the board to turn. A skater can alter the tightness of the trucks. Tightening the trucks makes it difficult to turn. Loosening the trucks makes turning easy.

The wheels are attached to the trucks. The skateboard's wheels can be different sizes. Small wheels work well if a skater wants to do tricks. But if speed is what the skater is after, large wheels are ideal.

The **bearings** are also important parts of the setup. The wheels revolve around the bearings. For this reason, bearings determine a skateboarder's speed and stability.

Each skateboard part is sold individually. This allows skaters to **custom build** their own skateboards. But a beginner can buy a board that is already assembled. This is less expensive and less confusing for someone new to the sport.

Style & Length

Skateboards come in three main lengths. Each length is best suited for a different style of skateboarding. So skaters must keep their skateboarding style in mind when selecting a board.

The mini board is perfect for beginners. It is 24 inches (61 cm) long. The mini board is easy to **maneuver** and exciting to ride. It is small, so even young skaters can use it to learn basic skills.

The mini board is often used in slalom racing. This is weaving around cones or other obstacles while skating down a hill. Because the mini board is easy to maneuver, it makes for a faster run.

The 27-inch (69-cm) skateboard is usually used for freestyle and downhill skateboarding. These boards are less **flexible** than others. For this reason, they support **stunts** better than other boards.

Freestyle skateboarders perform tricks on open ground. These tricks are done without ramps or jumps. Some people even perform gymnastic **routines** with their boards. Headstands and handstands are popular tricks in this skateboarding style.

The term flatland *is used to describe the open area used for freestyle tricks. This skater is performing a flatland ollie.*

15

Downhill skating may also be done on 27-inch (69-cm) boards. In downhill skating, skaters ride down steep hills as fast as they can. This can be dangerous, so only experienced skaters should try it. Skaters must always wear protective gear when downhill skating.

The 29- to 32-inch (74- to 81-cm) skateboards are often used for street and vert skating. These skateboards are wider than other boards. They are more difficult to turn, too. So only experienced skaters should use these boards.

The term *street skating* refers to people skating in the streets. Skaters use benches, curbs, and steps as tools for developing their **techniques**. Street skaters use longer skateboards because they are sturdier. This makes these boards good for the difficult moves of street skating.

The term *vert* is short for the word *vertical*. In vert skating, skaters use ramps of different heights, as well as other tools, to perform tricks.

Some skaters own more than one length of skateboard. This way, they can decide what style of skateboarding they want to do. Then they can choose the board for that style.

Starting Out

After selecting a skateboard, you are ready to skate! Make sure your protective gear is on properly and your helmet is secure.

To begin, find an area with no traffic. Your driveway or an empty parking lot are great places to learn. If you have a skatepark near your home, that is also a good place to start.

Next, decide which foot is most comfortable for pushing off. Place the other foot on the board's nose. Most people place their left foot on the nose and use their right foot to push. Doing the opposite is called skating goofy-footed. However, it does not mean you are doing it incorrectly.

After deciding where to place your feet, slowly push yourself around while on the board. When you are comfortable, give yourself a couple of strong pushes. Then, place both feet on the board. Your feet should be about shoulder-width apart.

It may take awhile to feel comfortable on your board. But at this point, you have already learned the basics! Soon, you will be able to learn new moves and perform cool tricks.

Opposite page: A goofy-footed stance

Tricks

kickturn

A skater can do a kickturn by pressing down with one foot on the skateboard's tail, while the other foot turns the board's nose in a different direction.

kickflip

A skater can do a kickflip by kicking the board while in midair, which causes the board to flip, and then landing on the deck.

aerial

An aerial is any trick performed in midair.

ollie

An ollie is a trick where the skateboard and the skater jump in the air, as if flying. It is a hard trick to learn, but it is the base for almost all other tricks. So skaters often learn this one first.

grind

To grind, a skater starts with an ollie. He or she then hops onto a curb or other object and grinds along the edge. This trick can be done with a number of different obstacles.

360

Doing a 360 means making a complete turn on a skateboard with either the front or back wheels off the ground.

Lingo

nose

The nose is the front of a skateboard.

skatepark

A skatepark is an area specifically set up for skaters to practice in. It can be either indoors or outdoors.

regular stance

Regular stance is skating with the left foot planted on the board's nose and pushing off with the right foot.

goofy-footed

Skating goofy-footed is placing the right foot on the board's nose and pushing off with the left foot.

skate

This is a game similar to the basketball game called Horse. A skater performs a trick, and a second skater has to land the same trick. If the second skater fails, he or she earns the letter s. The game continues until someone spells the word skate and loses.

sponsor

A sponsor is a company that provides a skater with money for wearing its clothing and using its equipment during competition.

signature-model skateboard

This is a skateboard that has been named after a specific skater.

tail

The tail is the back of a skateboard.

Tony Hawk

Today's most famous skateboarder is Tony Hawk. He was born in 1968. Hawk stepped on his first skateboard when he was eight years old. Hawk's father encouraged his son's ability.

Hawk became a **professional** skateboarder at age 14. By age 16, Hawk was the best skateboarder in the world. During his career, he entered more than 100 professional contests and won most of them.

In 1999, Hawk did a trick called a 900. A 900 is two and one-half spins done in the air with a skateboard before landing. He was the first person to land this trick.

Tony Hawk

Though Hawk has retired from his **professional** career, he still loves to skate. He often performs and does **demos**. He has accomplished tricks that few other skateboarders have even thought of trying. He has also invented several tricks of his own.

Tony Hawk performing in 1999

Skateboarding Today

Skateboarding is still popular today. People of all ages are learning to skate. In addition, many people who learned to skateboard as children are continuing to skateboard as adults.

Several skaters have become famous. Tom Penny, Danny Way, and Chad Muska compete **professionally**. They have spent many years practicing and performing at competitions all over the world.

There are several important skateboarding competitions. Skaters

can compete in the Gravity Games, the X Games, and the Globe World Cup. These and other competitions have helped skateboarding become popular around the world.

Today, there are millions of skateboarders. There are hundreds of skateparks, too. Unfortunately, many communities still do not have one. But every year, new skateparks are developed.

One of the best ways to learn to skateboard is to attend a camp. There, new skaters are able to practice on quality skateboarding equipment. They will also receive excellent training and learn new tricks. Advanced skaters may benefit from these camps as well.

Another way to learn is by watching **professionals** perform in skateboarding videos. These videos are fun to watch. They are also instructive. New skaters can learn basic **techniques**. Advanced skaters may learn new tricks.

Many magazines about skateboarding are available, too. In these magazines, skateboarders can learn about new tricks, new stars, and different contests.

Today, resources for skaters are everywhere. Hundreds of skaters, male and female, have proven their talents over the years. Every day, thousands of new skaters start practicing in the hopes that they, too, will achieve fame.

Glossary

bearing - a machine piece that supports a moving part, allowing it to move more smoothly.

custom build - to make something to fit the individual wants or needs of a single person.

demo - a term that is short for the word *demonstration*. A demo shows a product or activity by performing examples.

flexible - able to bend without breaking.

maneuver - to move or manage.

professional - working for money in an activity, such as a sport, that others participate in for entertainment.

routine - a series of moves worked out as part of a sports contest.

shock - the effect of a sudden impact.

stunt - an act that is done to attract attention, especially one showing strength, skill, or courage.

technique - a method used to perform an action or activity.

unique - being the only one of its kind.

urethane - a plastic.

Web Sites

Would you like to learn more about skateboarding? Please visit **www.abdopub.com** to find up-to-date Web site links about this sport and its competitions. These links are routinely monitored and updated to provide the most current information available.

Index